초등 영단어 500 따라쓰기

기획 : 와이앤엠 어학연구소

와이 앤 엠

차 례

초등 영단어
500
따라쓰기

1. 학생 · 학용품

bag
가방, 봉지

[bæg 백]

bag   bag   bag   bag

board
판자, 게시판

[bɔːrd 보-ㄹ드]

board   board   board   board

camp
캠프

[kæmp 캠프]

camp   camp   camp   camp

chalk
분필

[tʃɔːk 초어크]

chalk   chalk   chalk   chalk

· This is my schoolbag.　　　　　　이건 제 책가방이예요.

· What's this new board for?　　　이 새 게시판은 어디에 쓸 거죠?

· Let's go camping.　　　　　　　캠핑하러 가자.

· Let's buy blackboard and chalk.　칠판과 분필을 삽시다.

class
수업, 학급

[klæs 클래스]

class   class   class

computer
컴퓨터

[kəmpjúːtər
컴퓨-러ㄹ]

computer   computer

crayon
크레용

[kréiən
크래이언]

crayon   crayon   crayon

desk
책상

[desk 데스크]

desk   desk   desk   desk

eraser
지우개

[iréisəvər
이뢰이줘ㄹ]

eraser eraser eraser

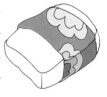

· It's time to finish the class.   수업을 끝낼 시간이예요.
· There are three compurters on the desk.   책상위에 컴퓨터가 3대 있어요.
· I like to draw lines using crayons.   크레용으로 선긋는 것을 좋아해요.
· There is a pencil on the desk.   책상 위에 연필 한 자루가 있어요.
· Tom, can I borrow your eraser?   Tom, 지우개 좀 빌려줄래?

learn
배우다

[ləːrn 러-ㄹ언]

learn　learn　learn　learn

lesson
수업

[lésn 렛쓴]

lesson lesson lesson lesson

library
도서관

[láibreri 라이브뢰뤼]

library　　library　　library

page
페이지, 쪽

[peidʒ 페이쥐]

page　page　page　page

pin
핀

[pin 핀]

pin　pin　pin　pin　pin　pin

- I want to learn English.　　　　　　전 영어를 배우고 싶어요.
- I have no lesson today.　　　　　　오늘은 수업이 하나도 없어요.
- Mom and I often go to a library.　엄마랑 저는 가끔 도서관에 가요.
- Open your page 6.　　　　　　　　6쪽을 펴세요.
- Please, lend me a safety pin.　　안전핀 좀 빌려 주시겠어요.

school
학교, 수업

[skuːl 스꾸-울]

school school school

student
학생

[stjúːdənt
스쮸-던트]

student student student

study
공부하다

[stʌ́di 스떠디]

study study study study

table
테이블

[téibl 테이블]

table table table

test
테스트

[test 테스트]

test test test test

- After school, I came back home.   수업이 끝난 후, 나는 집으로 돌아 왔어요.
- How many students are there?   학생이 몇 명 있죠?
- At school, I study English.   학교에서, 나는 영어를 공부한다.
- There are two books on the table.   테이블 위에 책이 2권 있다.
- I had a test last Friday.   지난 금요일에 나는 시험을 봤다.

2. 스포츠 · 예능

art
미술, 예술

[ɑːrt 알트]

art art art art art art

ball
공

[bɔːl 버-얼]

ball ball ball ball ball ball

camera
카메라

[kǽmərə캐므러]

camera camera

club
클럽, 동호회

[klʌb 클럽]

club club club club club

· My favorite subject is art.   내가 가장 좋아하는 과목은 미술이다.

· This is my sister's ball.   이건 우리 누나의 공이예요.

· I want to buy a new digital camera.   새 디지털카메라를 사고 싶어요.

· He is my club friend.   그는 내 동호회 친구야.

exercise
운동, 연습

[éksərsáiz
엑썰싸이즈]

exercise   exercise

dance
춤, 춤추다

[dæns 댄스]

dance dance dance

drum
북, 드럼

[drʌm 드럼]

drum   drum   drum   drum

film
필름, 영화

[film 필름]

film   film   film   film

game
게임

[geim 게임]

game game game game

- It's important to exercise everyday.   매일 운동하는 것은 중요해요.
- I like to dance.   저는 춤추는 걸 좋아해요.
- Peter is playing the drum.   Peter가 드럼을 치고 있어요.
- My parents like to go to see a film.   부모님은 영화보는 것을 좋아하세요.
- I like to play computer games.   컴퓨터 게임 하는 거 좋아해요.

guitar
기타

[gitá:r 기타-ㄹ]

guitar guitar guitar guitar

movie
영화

[mú:vi 무-뷔]

movie movie movie movie

music
음악

[mjú:zik 뮤-직]

music music music

piano
피아노

[piǽnou 애노우]

piano piano piano

sing
노래, 노래하다

[siŋ 씽]

sing sing sing sing sing

- Can you play the guitar?   기타 칠 줄 아세요?
- I went to the movie with my friends.   나는 친구들과 영화를 보러 갔다.
- I like listening to music.   나는 음악 듣는 것을 좋아한다.
- I can play the piano.   나는 피아노 연주를 할 수 있어요.
- My hobby is to sing songs.   내 취미는 노래 부르는 것이다.

skate
스케이트
[skeit스케잇-ㅌ]

skate skate skate skate

soccer
축구
[sákər싸커ㄹ]

soccer soccer soccer

song
노래
[sɔːŋ 썽]

song song song song

sport
스포츠
[spɔːrt스포-올트]

sport sport sport sport

swim
수영하다, 수영
[swim 스윔]

swim swim swim

- Let's go skating!
- I played soccer with my friends.
- I sang a song for my parents.
- Soccer is a popular sport in korea.
- We went swimming last Sunday.

스케이트 타러가자!
나는 친구들과 축구를 했어요.
나는 부모님을 위해 노래를 불렀어요.
한국에서 축구는 인기가 좋다.
지난 일요일 우리는 수영하러 갔다.

swing
그네

[swiŋ 스윙]

swing swing swing swing

team
팀

[tiːm 팀]

team team team team

tennis
테니스

[ténis 테니스]

tennis tennis tennis tennis

video
비디오

[vídioú
브이디오]

video video video

violin
바이올린

[váiəlín
봐이얼린]

violin violin violin

- There are two boys on the swing.   그네에 남자아이 둘이 타고 있다.
- His team won the game.   그의 팀이 게임에서 이겼다.
- She played tennis with her friend.   그녀는 친구와 함께 테니스를 쳤다.
- How often do you rent video tapes?   당신은 얼마나 자주 비디오 테이프를 빌려요?
- I can play the violin.   저는 바이올린을 연주할 수 있어요.

12

3. 과 일

apple
사과
[ǽpəl 애쁠]

apple apple apple

banana
바나나
[bənǽnə 버내너]

banana banana

cabbage
양배추
[kǽbidʒ 캐비지]

cabbage cabbage cabbage

carrot
당근
[kǽrət 캐럿]

carrot carrot carrot carrot

- Do you like apples? 사과 좋아하세요?
- I like bananas very much. 나는 바나나를 무척 좋아해요.
- The man is chopping up the cabbage. 남자는 양배추를 썰고 있다.
- My hamster likes to eat carrots. 내 햄스터는 당근을 즐겨 먹는다.

cucumber
오이

[kjú:kʌmbər 큐컴벌]

cucumber   cucumber

fruit
과일

[fru:t푸룻-ㅌ]

fruit fruit fruit fruit fruit

grape
포도

[greip 그뢰입]

grape   grape   grape

melon
메론

[mélən메런]

melon melon melon melon

onion
양파

[ʌ́njən어니언]

onion   onion   onion   onion

- A cucumber is long and green. 오이는 길고 녹색이다.
- What is your favorite fruit? 좋아하는 과일이 무엇인가요?
- Does Peter like grapes? Peter는 포도를 좋아하나요?
- Melons are in full flush. 멜론이 한물졌다.
- Hold the onions with my burger. 제 버거에는 양파를 생략해 주세요.

peach
복숭아
[piːtʃ
피-치]

peach peach peach peach

pear
(과일)배
[pɛəʳ 페얼]

pear   pear   pear   pear

pineapple
파인애플
[páinæpl 파인애쁠]

pineapple   pineapple

strawberry
딸기
[strɔ́ːbéri
스뜨뤄-베뤼]

strawberry   strawberry

tomato
토마토
[təméitqu
터메이토]

tomato   tomato   tomato

- I'm allergic to peaches.   나는 복숭아 알레르기가 있어요.
- This pear is sweet.   이 배는 달다.
- Do you like eating pineapples?   여러분은 파인애플 먹는 것을 좋아하나요?
- I like strawberry.   나는 딸기를 좋아해요.
- My mother likes tomato juice.   엄마는 토마토주스를 좋아하세요.

4. 음식

butter
버터
[bʌ́tər 버러ㄹ]

butter butter butter butter

breakfast
아침식사
[brékfəst 브뢰ㄱ퓌스트]

breakfast breakfast

bread
빵
[bred 브레드]

bread bread bread

cake
케이크
[keik 케이크]

cake cake cake cake

- There are bread and butter.　　　　빵과 버터가 있어요.
- I ate bread and milk for breakfast.　나는 아침으로 빵과 우유를 먹었다.
- Tom, would like some bread?　　　　Tom, 빵 좀 먹을래?
- She gave me a piece of cake.　　　　그녀는 나에게 케이크 한 조각을 주었다.

candy
사탕

[kǽndi 캔디]

candy candy candy

cheese
치즈

[tʃiːz 취-즈]

cheese cheese cheese

corn
옥수수

[kɔːrn 콘]

corn corn corn corn corn

cream
크림

[kriːm 크뤼-임]

cream cream cream

dinner
저녁 식사

[dínər 디널]

dinner dinner dinner

- Andy gave me a candy.
- Mice are eating cheese.
- Do you like corn?
- Put two spoons of cream.
- I had dinner with my friend, Tony.

Andy가 나에게 사탕을 주었어요.
쥐들이 치즈를 먹고 있어요.
옥수수 좋아하세요?
크림 두 스푼을 넣으세요.
나는 친구 Tony와 저녁을 먹었어요.

17

egg
달걀

[eg 엑]

egg   egg   egg   egg

food
음식

[fu:d 푸-드]

food   food   food   food

hamburger
햄버거

[hǽmbəːrgər햄버거]

hamburger   hamburger

Juice
주스

[dʒúːs 쥬-스]

juice   juice   juice

meat
고기

[miːt 미-잇트]

meat   meat   meat   meat

- Chickens lay an egg each morning.
- What is your favorite food?
- Are you eating hamburger again?
- Would you like some juice?
- We will have meat for dinner.

닭은 매일 아침 달걀을 한 개씩 낳아요.
좋아하는 음식은 무엇인가요?
너 햄버거 또 먹는거야?
주스 좀 드실래요?
우리는 저녁식사로 고기를 먹을 거야.

milk
우유
[milk 밀크]

milk milk milk milk

rice
쌀, 밥
[rais 롸이스]

rice rice rice rice rice

salad
샐러드
[sǽləd 쌜러드]

salad salad salad

salt
소금
[sɔːlt 써-얼트]

salt salt salt salt salt

sugar
설탕
[ʃúgər 슈걸]

sugar sugar sugar sugar

- Milk is good for our health.
- Korean usually eat rice.
- I ate some salad and chicken.
- Could you pass me the salt, please.
- Do you like sugar in your coffee?

우유는 건강에 좋다.
한국 사람들은 보통 밥을 먹는다.
나는 샐러드와 치킨을 먹었다.
소금 좀 건내 주시겠어요?
커피에 설탕 넣으시겠어요?

5. 자 연

air
공기

[εər 에어ㄹ]

air air air air air

beach
물가, 바닷가

[biːtʃ 비-잇취]

beach beach beach beach

cloud
구름

[klaud클라우드]

cloud cloud cloud

earth
지구, 땅

[əːrθ어-ㄹ쓰]

earth earth earth earth

· We would die without air.   우리는 공기가 없으면 죽고 말 거야.

· We will go to beach.   나는 올 여름 바닷가에 가고 싶어요.

· The birds fly over the clouds.   새들이 구름 위로 날아다녀요.

· There are a lot of animals on the earth.   지구에는 많은 동물들이 있어요.

grass
풀
[græs 그뢰쓰]

grass   grass   grass   grass

lake
호수
[leik 레익]

lake   lake   lake   lake

mountain
산
[mauntən마운튼]

mountain   mountain

plant
식물
[plænt 플랜트]

plant   plant   plant   plant

rainbow
무지개
[réinbóu
뢰인보우]

rainbow   rainbow   rainbow

- "Keep off the grass."   잔디에 들어가지 마시오.
- There are many lakes in Canada.   캐나다에는 호수가 많아요.
- I climbed a mountain last Saturday.   나는 지난 토요일 산에 올랐어요.
- The plants need water.   식물은 물이 필요하다.
- we can see a rainbow after it rains.   비가 오고 난 후에는 무지개를 볼 수 있다.

river
강

[rívər 뤼버-ㄹ]

river   river   river

sand
모래

[sænd 쌘드]

sand   sand   sand   sand

sea
바다

[si: 씨-]

sea   sea   sea   sea

silver
은, 은빛, 은의

[sílvər 씰뷔얼]

silver   silver   silver   silver

snow
눈, 눈이오다

[snou 스노우]

snow   snow   snow

- I jumped into the river.   나는 강에 뛰어 들었어요.
- We built sand castles.   우리는 모래성을 쌓았다.
- I went to the sea last summer.   나는 지난 여름에 바다에 갔어요.
- He gave me a silver ring.   그는 나에게 은반지를 주었다.
- It is snowing.   눈이 오고 있다.

space
공간, 우주

[speis 스뻬이스]

space space space space

star
별

[staːr 스따-ㄹ]

star star star star

sun
태양, 햇빛

[sʌn 썬]

sun sun sun sun sun

water
물

[wɔ́ːtər 워-터]

water water water

wind
바람

[wind 윈드]

wind wind wind

- The people are looking for a parking space.　사람들이 주차할 공간을 찾고 있다.
- It is hard to see stars in the city.　도시에서는 별을 보기 힘들다.
- The sun rises in the east.　해는 동쪽에서 뜬다.
- People drink water every day.　사람들은 물을 매일 마신다.
- The paper is swing in the wind.　그 종이가 바람에 흔들린다.

6. 동 물

animal
동물, 짐승

[ǽnəməl 애니멀]

animal   animal   animal

ant
개미

[ænt 앤트]

ant   ant   ant   ant

bird
새

[bəːrd 버얼드]

bird   bird   bird   bird

chicken
닭

[tʃíkən 취킨]

chicken   chicken   chicken

- A bear is a big animal.   곰은 몸집이 큰 동물이에요.
- The ants are diligent.   개미들은 부지런하다.
- Birds fly in the air.   새들은 공중을 날아다녀요.
- The chickens make a lot of noise.   닭들이 너무나 시끄럽게 해요.

cow
암소, 젖소

[kau 카우]

cow   cow   cow   cow

deer
사슴

[diər 디얼]

deer   deer   deer

duck
오리

[dʌk 덕]

duck   duck   duck   duck

elephant
코끼리

[éləfənt엘러풔ㄴ트]

elephant   elephant

fish
물고기

[fiʃ 퓌쉬]

fish   fish   fish   fish

- Cows make milk.   암소들은 우유를 만들어요.
- Have you ever seen a deer?   사슴을 본 적이 있니?
- The ducks can't fly.   오리는 날 수 없다.
- The elephants are very strong.   코끼리는 매우 힘이 세다.
- Did you catch any fish?   고기 좀 잡으셨어요?

25

fly(2)
파리

[flai 플라이]

fly fly fly fly fly fly

fox
여우

[faks]

fox fox fox fox fox fox

hen
암탉

[hen 헨]

hen hen hen hen

horse
말

[hɔːrs 호올스]

horse horse horse

monkey
원숭이

[mʌ́ŋki 멍끼]

monkey monkey

- Frog eats fly.   개구리는 파리를 먹어요.
- A fox is a wild animal.   여우는 야생 동물이다.
- Hen lays an egg.   암탉은 계란을 낳아요.
- Riding a horse is very funny.   말타는 건 재밌어요.
- Monkeys like bananas.   원숭이들은 바나나를 좋아해요.

pig
돼지

[pig 픽]

pig pig pig pig pig

sheep
양

[ʃiːp 쉽]

sheep sheep sheep sheep

tiger
호랑이

[táigər 타이걸]

tiger tiger tiger

zoo
동물원

[zuː 주-]

zoo zoo zoo zoo zoo zoo

- Pigs eat a lot.   돼지는 많이 먹어요.
- I have never seen a sheep.   나는 양을 본 적이 없어요.
- Have you ever seen a tiger?   너는 호랑이를 본 적 있니?
- Let's go to the zoo.   동물원에 가자.

7. 색

black
검은 색
[blæk 블랙]

black black black black

blue
파란색
[blu: 블루-]

blue blue blue

brown
갈색, 갈색의
[braun 브롸운]

brown brown brown

color
색깔
[kʌ́lər 컬러ㄹ]

color color color color

- The prince has black hair.　　　왕자 머리카락은 검은색이에요.
- Jessica has blue eyes.　　　Jessica의 눈은 파란색이예요.
- My teacher wears brown jacket.　　　선생님은 갈색 자켓을 입고 계시다.
- What is your favorite color?　　　가장 좋아하는 색이 뭐야?

gray
회색, 회색의

[grei 그뢰이]

gray　　gray　　gray　　gray

pink
분홍

[piŋk 핑크]

pink　　pink　　pink　　pink

red
빨간색, 붉은

[red 뢰드]

red　red　red　red　red　red

white
흰, 흰빛

[hwait 와이트]

white　white　white　white

yellow
노랑

[jélou 옐로-]

yellow　　　　yellow

- I like this gray sweater.　나는 이 회색 스웨터가 좋아.
- I like the pink.　나는 분홍색을 좋아해요.
- She was red with shame.　그녀는 부끄러워서 얼굴이 빨개졌다.
- We can see the white color in the dark.　우리는 어둠 속에서 흰색을 볼 수 있다.
- The banana is yellow.　바나나는 노랑색이다.

8. 나 · 너 · 우리

he
그는, 그가

[hiː 히-]

he he he he he

her
그녀의

[həːr 허얼]

her her her her

hers
그녀의 것

[həːrz 허어즈]

hers hers hers

him
그를, 그에게

[him 힘]

him him him him him

· He pointed the girl with a doll.

그는 인형을 가지고 있는 그 소녀를 가르켰어요.

· Jane is doing her homework.

Jane은 숙제하고 있어요.

· This comic book is hers.

이 만화책은 그녀의 것이야.

· She loves him.

그녀는 그를 사랑해요.

his
그의, 그의 것

[híz 히이스]

his his his his his

I
나는, 내가

[ai 아이]

I I I I I I I I

it
그것은

[it 잇]

it it it it it it it it

its
그것의

[its 잇즈]

its its its its its its its its

me
나를

[mi 미-]

me me me me me me

· It is his umbrella. 그것은 그의 우산이야.
· I'm peter. I'm 10years old. 나는 Peter예요. 10살이죠.
· It is your dog. 그것은 당신의 강아지예요.
· The baby is sleeping in its bed. 갓난 아기는 침대에서 자고 있어요.
· Look at me! 나를 보세요.

mine
나의 것
[máin 마인]

mine   mine   mine   mine

my
나의
[mái 마이]

my   my   my   my   my

our
우리의
[auər 아우월]

our our our our our our

ours
우리의 것
[auərz 아워즈]

ours   ours   ours   ours

she
그녀는, 그녀가
[ʃiː 쉬]

she   she   she   she

- The pen is mine.   그 펜은 내거야.
- This is my digital camera.   이것은 제 디지털카메라예요.
- That building is our school.   저 건물이 우리 학교야.
- Which car is ours?   어느 것이 우리 차냐?
- She is really beautiful.   그녀는 정말 아름다워요.

that
저것, 그것
[ðæt 댓]

that that that that

the
그
[ðə/ði 더/디]

the the the the the the

their
그들의
[ðɛər 데얼]

their their their their

them
그들을
[ðem 뎀]

them them them

there
거기에
[ðɛər 데얼]

there there there there

- Look at that! That is big!
- The girl is my sister.
- Their captain is very good.
- I told them to wait.
- Look over there.

저것좀 봐! 크다!
그 소녀는 내 여동생입니다.
그들의 주장은 굉장히 좋은 사람이야.
나는 그들에게 기다리라고 말했어요.
저기 좀 봐.

these
이것들

[ðíːz 디-즈]

these　these　these

they
그들은

[ðei 데이]

they　they　they

this
이것

[ðis 디쓰]

this this this this this this

those
그것들

[ðouz 도즈]

those　those　those　those

us
우리들을

[ʌs 어쓰]

us us us us us us us us

- These apples are red. 　　　　　　이 사과들은 빨갛다.
- They are going to school. 　　　　그들은 학교에 가고 있어요.
- How about this shirt? 　　　　　　이 셔츠는 어때요?
- Those shoes are expensive. 　　　그 구두는 비싸다.
- He told us to stay home. 　　　　그는 우리에게 집에 있으라고 했다.

we
우리, 저희가

[wiː 위-]

you
너, 당신

[juː 유-]

your
너의, 너희들의

[juəʳ 유얼]

yours
너의 것

[juəʳz 유어즈]

- We go to school at 8 o'clock.　　우리는 8시에 등교한다.
- You look so pretty.　　너는 굉장히 예쁘다(너는 참 예쁘구나).
- What is your name?　　너의 이름은 무엇이니?
- Yours is beautiful.　　너의 것은 예쁘다.

9. 가 족

baby
아기
[béibi베이비]

baby   baby   baby   baby

cousin
사촌, 친척
[kʌ́zn커즌]

cousin   cousin   cousin

dad/daddy
아빠
[dæd대드]

dad   dad   dad   dad   dad

daughter
딸
[dɔ́:tər더-러]

daughter   daughter

- The baby girl is my little sister.   그 여자 아기는 내 여동생이예요.
- This is my cousin, Mike.   얘는 내 사촌 Mike야.
- Dad reads me some books at night.   아빠는 밤에 저에게 책을 읽어주셔요.
- My aunt has two daughters and a son.   우리 이모는 1남 2녀(아들한명과 두 딸)를 두셨어요.

family
가족

[fǽməli 페믈리]

family family

mom
엄마

[mam 맘]

mom mom mom mom

parent
부모님

[pɛ̀ərənt
페어뤄ㄴ트]

parent parent parent

son
아들

[sɔn 썬]

son son son son son

uncle
아저씨, 삼촌

[ʌ́ŋkl 엉끌]

uncle uncle uncle

- This is a picture of my family.　우리 가족 사진이예요.
- Mom got angry with me.　어머니가 나에게 화가 나셨다.
- My parents are very nice.　나의 부모님은 매우 좋으신 분이예요.
- He is my son.　그는 나의 아들이다.
- I am going to my uncle's.　나는 삼촌댁에 갈 거예요.

mom
엄마

[mam 맘]

mom　mom　mom　mom

mother
어머니

[mʌ́ðər 머덜]

mother　mother

sister
여자형제, 언니

[sístər 씨스털]

sister　sister　sister

son
아들

[sɔn 썬]

son　son　son　son　son

- Mom got angry with me.　　　　어머니가 나에게 화가 나셨다.

- She is my mother.　　　　그녀는 나의 어머니예요.

- I have two sisters.　　　　나는 두 명의 여자형제가 있어요.

- He is my son.　　　　그는 나의 아들이다.

10. 우리 몸

arm
팔
[aːrm 아-ㄹ암]

arm   arm   arm   arm

back
등, 뒤
[bæk 백]

back   back   back   back

body
몸, 신체
[bádi 바디]

body   body   body

ear
귀
[iər 이얼]

ear ear ear ear ear ear

- Tom's arm is long.   Tom은 팔이 길어요.
- I looked at his back.   난 그의 등을 보았어요.
- My whole body is aching now.   지금 온몸이 아파요.
- Rabbits have long ears.   토끼의 귀는 길어요.

eye
눈

[ai 아이]

eye   eye   eye   eye   eye

face
얼굴

[feis페 이스]

face face face face

finger
손가락

[fíŋgər 휭거ㄹ]

finger finger finger

foot
발

[fut 풋]

foot foot foot

hair
머리카락, 털

[hɛər 헤얼]

hair hair hair hair hair

- Open your eyes and look around.
- I wash my face everyday.
- I touched water with my fingers.
- Peter is pushing the box with his foot.
- Her hair is black and short.

눈을 뜨고 주위를 둘러보세요.
나는 매일 얼굴을 씻어요(세수해요).
손가락으로 물을 만져보았어요.
Peter는 발로 상자를 밀고 있다.
그녀의 머리카락은 검고 짧아.

hand
손
[hænd 핸드]

hand hand hand hand

head
머리
[hed 헤드]

head head head

heart
마음, 심장
[haːrt 하-르트]

heart heart heart heart

knee
무릎
[niː 니-]

knee knee knee

leg
다리
[leg 렉]

leg leg leg leg leg

- We must wash our hands. 손을 꼭 씻어야 해요.
- His head touches the ceiling. 그의 머리는 천장에 닿아요.
- The doctor is checking my heart. 의사 선생님이 제 심장을 검사하고 계세요.
- I feel pain in my knee. 무릎이 아파요.
- I broke my leg three days ago. 3일전에 다리가 부러졌어요.

lip
입술

[lip 립]

lip   lip   lip   lip   lip   lip

mouth
입

[mauθ 마웃쓰]

mouth   mouth

neck
목

[nek 넥]

neck   neck   neck   neck

nose
코

[nouz노우즈]

nose   nose   nose

tooth
이, 치아

[tuːθ 투-쓰]

tooth   tooth   tooth   tooth

- Her lips turned purple with cold.   추워서 그의 입술이 자줏빛이 되었다.
- Tom opened his mouth.   Tom은 입을 벌렸어요.
- A neck is a part of our body.   목은 우리 몸의 한 부분이다.
- We have a nose.   우리는 하나의 코를 가지고 있다.
- Brush your tooth before you go to bed.   자기전 이를 닦아라.

11. 집 · 가구

apartment
아파트
[əpáːrtmənt
아파-알트먼트]

apartment   apartment

basket
바구니
[bǽskit 배스킷]

basket   basket   basket

bell
종, 초인종
[bel 벨]

bell bell bell bell bell bell

bench
긴 의자, 벤치
[bentʃ 벤취]

bench bench bench bench

- I really like my apartment.   나는 우리 아파트가 정말 좋아요.
- What do you have in your basket?   바구니 안에 뭐가 있어요?
- Listen! The bell is ringing.   들어봐~ 종이 울리고 있어.
- There are three benches in the park.   공원에는 벤치가 3개 있다.

chair
의자

[tʃɛər 췌어ㄹ]

chair　chair　chair

cup
컵

[kʌp 컵]

cup　cup　cup　cup　cup

curtain
커튼

[kə́ːrtn 커튼]

curtain　curtain　curtain

dish
접시

[diʃ 디쉬]

dish　dish　dish　dish

door
문

[dɔːr 도얼]

door　door　door　door

- There is a cat under the chair.　의자 밑에 고양이 한 마리가 있어요.
- I bought this cup for mom.　나는 엄마 드리려고 이 컵을 샀어요.
- I hid behind the curtain.　전 커튼 뒤로 숨었어요.
- I sometimes help mom to wash the dishes.　저는 가끔 엄마가 설거지하는 것을 도와드려요.
- I knocked on the door.　나는 문을 두드렸어요.

garden
정원

[gáːrdn 가-ㄹ든]

garden   garden   garden

gas
가스

[gæs 개스]

gas   gas   gas   gas

glass
유리, 유리컵

[glæs 글래쓰]

glass   glass   glass   glass

home
집

[hóum 홈]

home   home   home   home

kitchen
부엌

[kítʃin 킷췬]

kitchen   kitchen

- There are roses in that garden.　　저 정원엔 장미가 있어요.
- We filled the ballon with gas.　　우리는 풍선에 가스를 채웠다.
- I drink three glasses of milk everyday.　　나는 매일 우유를 세 잔씩 마셔요.
- I have to stay at home today.　　나는 오늘 집에 있어야만 해요.
- Refrigerator is in the kitchen.　　냉장고는 부엌에 있어요.

knife
칼
[naif 나이프]

knife knife knife knife

mirror
거울
[mírər미뤄-ㄹ]

mirror mirror mirror

roof
지붕
[ruːf 루-프]

roof roof roof roof roof

room
방
[ruːm 루-움]

room room room

soap
비누
[soup 쏘웁]

soap soap soap soap

- · The knife is dangerous.   그 칼은 위험해요.
- · She stands before a mirror all day.   그녀는 하루 종일 거울 앞에 서 있다.
- · Our house has a red roof.   우리집에는 빨간 지붕이 있다.
- · I usually study in my room.   나는 보통 내 방에서 공부해요.
- · Wash your hand with soap.   비누로 손을 깨끗이 씻어라.

sofa
소파

[sóufə쏘우풔]

spoon
숟가락, 스푼

[spuːn스푸-ㄴ]

stair
계단

[stɛər 스떼어]

telephone
전화

[téləfóun
텔레포운]

window
창(창문)

[wíndou윈도우]

- The cushion is on the sofa.
- I ate my meal with a spoon.
- I went up stairs.
- He is on the telephone.
- Please open the window.

그 쿠션은 소파 위에 있다.
나는 숟가락으로 식사를 했다.
나는 계단을 올랐다.
그는 통화중이다.
창문 좀 열어 주세요.

12. 직 업

captain
선장, 우두머리

[kǽptin 캡틴]

captain captain captain

cook
요리사

[kúk 쿡]

cook cook cook

doctor
의사

[dάktər닥터ㄹ]

doctor doctor doctor

farmer
농부

[fάːrmər파ー머ー]

farmer farmer farmer

- Mr. Han is the captain of the soccer team.
  한선생님은 그 축구팀의 주장이에요.

- My mom is a great cook.
  우리 엄마는 훌륭한 요리사다.

- I would like to be a doctor.
  나는 의사가 되고 싶어요.

- The farmer loves art.
  농부는 예술을 사랑한답니다.

fisherman
어부

[fíʃərmən 피셔-먼]

fisherman   fisherman

job
일, 직업

[dʒab 좝]

job job job job job job

nurse
간호사

[nəːrs 널쓰]

nurse nurse nurse

pilot
조종사

[páilət 파일럿]

pilot pilot pilot pilot pilot

police
경찰

[pəlíːs 펄리-스]

police police police

- The fisherman launched.   그 어부는 고기를 잡으러 갔다.
- "What's her job?"   그녀의 직업은 무엇인가요?
- She is a nurse.   그녀는 간호사이다.
- I want to be a pilot.   나는 조종사가 되고 싶어요.
- Police caught a thief.   경찰이 도둑을 잡았어요.

reporter
기자

[ripɔ́ːrtər
리포-터-]

reporter reporter reporter

scientist
과학자

[sáiəntist
사이언티스트]

scientist scientist

stewardess
스튜어디스

[stjúːərdis
스튜어디스]

stewardess stewardess

talent
탤런트

[tǽlənt파-머-]

talent talent talent talent

- This is a reporter of the CNN.　　　저는 CNN의 기자입니다.
- He is an eminent scientist.　　　　그는 훌륭한 과학자입니다.
- I want to be a stewardess.　　　　저는 스튜어디스가 되고 싶습니다.
- He is well-known talent.　　　　　그는 유명한 탤런트입니다.

13. 옷

cap
모자

[kæp 캡]

cap cap cap cap

coat
외투

[kout 코웃]

coat coat coat coat coat

dress
의복

[dres 드뢰스]

dress dress dress

pants
바지

[pænts 팬츠]

pants pants pants pants

- Mom bought me this cap.　　　　　엄마가 이 모자를 사주셨어요.
- My grandfather bought me a blue coat.　　할아버지께서 파란색 코트를 사주셨어요.
- My grandfather bought me a blue coat.　　할아버지께서 파란색 코트를 사주셨어요.
- I want to wear the pink dress.　　분홍색 드레스(옷)를 입고 싶어요.

ring
반지

[riŋ 링]

ring　ring　ring　ring

shoe
신, 구두

[ʃuː 슈-]

shoe　shoe　shoe　shoe

skirt
스커트

[skəːrt 스꺼얼트]

skirt　skirt　skirt

sweater
스웨터

[swétər 스웨터]

sweater　sweater　sweater

umbrella
우산

[ʌmbrélə 엄브뤨러]

umbrella　umbrella

- He gave me a ring.   그가 나에게 반지를 주었어요.
- My father bought a pair of shoes for me.   아빠가 저에게 신발(한켤레)을 사주셨어요.
- That skirt looks cool.   저 치마 멋져보여.
- This sweater is warm.   이 스웨터는 따뜻하다.
- He has an umbrella in his hand.   그의 손에 우산이 있다(그는 우산을 들고 있어요).

14. 건 물

airport
공항
[ɛ́ərpɔ̀:rt
에어포-르트]

airport   airport

bank
은행
[bæŋk 뱅크]

bank   bank   bank   bank

bridge
다리
[bridʒ 브릿쥐]

bridge   bridge

capital
수도, 서울
[kǽpitl캐피틀]

capital   capital   capital

- Is there a bus to airport?　　　공항으로 가는 버스가 있어요?
- My father works for that bank.　우리 아빠는 저 은행에서 일하셔요.
- We walked across the bridge.　우리는 걸어서 다리를 건넜어요.
- Seoul is the capital of Korea.　서울은 대한민국의 수도예요.

church
교회

[tʃɚːtʃ 춰-ㄹ춰]

church   church

city
도시

[síti 씨티]

city city city city city city

floor
바닥, 층

[flɔːr 플로-월]

floor   floor   floor   floor

hospital
병원

[háspitl 하스피틀]

hospital hospital hospital

hotel
호텔

[houtél 호텔]

hotel hotel hotel hotel

- I go to church on Sundays.   저는 일요일마다 교회에 가요.
- There are lots of people in the city.   이 도시에는 사람들이 아주 많아요.
- The book store is on the third floor.   그 서점은 3층에 있어요.
- Ted is in the hospital.   Ted는 병원에 입원해 있어요.
- How about staying in a hotel?   호텔에 묵는 건 어때요?

office
사무실

[ɔ́ːfis어-퓌스]

picnic
소풍

[píknik피크닉]

place
장소, 곳

[pleis플레이스]

restaurant
레스토랑

[résterənt
뢰스토뤈트드]

road
길, 도로

[roud 로우드]

- He works hard in his office. 그는 그의 사무실에서 열심히 일한다.
- We went on a picnic last weekend. 우리는 지난 주말에 소풍을 갔다.
- The place is very nice. 그 장소는 매우 멋져.
- We had a dinner at restaurant. 우리는 레스토랑에서 저녁을 먹었어요.
- The road is narrow. 그 도로는 좁아요.

station
역, 정거장

[stéiʃən 스떼이션]

station   station

street
거리

[strit 스프뤼-ㅅ]

street   street   street   street

travel
여행, 여행하다

[trǽvəl 튜뢰블]

travel   travel   travel   travel

trip
여행

[trip 츄뤄ㅂ]

trip   trip   trip   trip

- **I wait for taxi at the** station.   나는 정거장에서 택시를 기다린다.

- **Let's cross the** street.   길을 건너자.

- **I want to** travel **around the world.**   나는 전세계를 여행하고 싶어요.

- **How was your** trip?   이거 해보자!(이거 시도해보자)

15. 탈 것

airplane
비행기
[ɛ́ərplén
에얼플레인]

airplane　airplane　airplane

ambulance
구급차
[ǽmb앰뷸런스]

ambulance　　ambulance

bicycle
자전거
[báisikəl바이시클]

bicycle　　bicycle

boat
보트, 작은배
[bout 보웃트]

boat　boat　boat　boat

- I go to Busan by airplane.　　나는 부산에 비행기로 간다.
- The ambulance is arriving.　　구급차가 도착하고 있다.
- Can you ride a bicycle?　　자전거를 탈 수 있나요?
- My uncle has a big boat.　　삼촌은 큰 보트를 가지고 계신다.

ship
배

[ʃip 쉽]

ship   ship   ship   ship

sled
썰매

[sled 슬레드]

sled   sled   sled   sled   sled

subway
지하철

[sʌ́bwéi 써브웨이]

subway   subway

train
기차

[trein 츄뢰인]

train   train   train

truck
트럭

[trʌk 츄럭]

truck   truck   truck   truck

- Look at that ship!
- In winter, we sled.
- We went to In-cheon by subway.
- I will travel by train.
- The truck is big.

저 배를 봐요!
겨울에 우리는 썰매를 탄다.
우리는 지하철로 인천에 갔다.
나는 기차로 여행할거예요.
저 트럭은 크다.

16. 때 · 계절

afternoon
오후

[æftərnúːn
애프터ㄹ누-운]

afternoon afternoon

autumn
가을

[óːtəm 어-틈]

autumn autumn

date
날짜

[deit 데잇트]

date date date

day
낮, 하루

[dei 데이]

day day day day day day

- I met him in the afternoon.　　　나는 그를 오후에 만났어요.

- It is windy in the autumn.　　　가을에는 바람이 많이 불어요.

- What's the date today?　　　오늘 몇일이에요?(오늘 날짜가 어떻게 되죠?)

- I play all day long every day.　　　난 매일 하루 종일 놀아요.

evening
저녁

[íːvniŋ 이-브닝]

evening   evening

fall
가을

[fɔːl 풔ㄹ]

fall fall fall fall fall fall

hour
시간

[auər 아우월]

hour   hour   hour

lunch
점심

[lɔntʃ 런취]

lunch lunch lunch lunch

morning
아침

[mɔ́ːrniŋ 모-ㄹ닝]

morning   morning

- I feel tired in the evening.   나는 저녁에는 피곤해.
- In fall, we can see many leaves.   가을에는 낙엽을 많이 볼 수 있어요.
- Peter slept for five hours.   Peter는 5시간동안 잤어요.
- It's time for lunch.   점심 먹을 시간이에요.
- Good morning!   좋은 아침!

night
밤

[nait 나잇]

night night night

noon
정오, 한 낮

[nuːn 눈]

noon noon noon noon

season
계절

[síːzn 씨-즌]

season season season

spring
봄

[spriŋ 스프링]

spring spring spring

summer
여름

[sámər 써머ㄹ]

summer summer summer

- I stayed up all night.   나는 밤새도록 깨어 있었다.
- We have lunch at noon.   우리는 정오에 점심을 먹는다.
- What's your favorite season?   가장 좋아하는 계절은?
- I like spring.   난 봄이 좋아요.
- In summer, it is hot.   여름에는 더워요.

today
오늘
[tudéi 투데이]

today today today today

tomorrow
내일
[təmɔ́:rou 투머-로우]

tomorrow tomorrow

week
주, 1주간
[wi:k 위-크]

week week week week

winter
겨울
[wíntər 윈터얼]

winter winter winter

yesterday
어제
[jéstərdéi 예스털데이]

yesterday yesterday

- Today is my birthday.　　　　　　오늘은 내 생일이다.
- Tomorrow will be cold.　　　　　내일은 추울 거야.
- I will travel America for a week.　나는 일주일동안 미국을 여행할 거야.
- It's cold in winter.　　　　　　　겨울엔 추워요.
- Yesterday was my brother's birthday.　어제는 내 남동생의 생일이었다.

62

17. 방향 · 길

east
동쪽

[i:st 이스트]

map
지도

[mæp 맵]

north
북쪽

[nɔ:rθ 노-ㄹ쓰]

south
남쪽

[sauθ 싸웃쓰]

. Go east. 동쪽으로 가.

. I marked my house on the map. 우리(나의)집을 지도에 표시했다.

· My house stands in the north of Seoul. 우리 집은 서울의 북쪽에 있다.

· The man went south. 그는 남쪽으로 갔다.

visit
방문하다

[vízit 뷔짓]

visit   visit   visit   visit

way
길, 방법

[wei 웨이]

way   way   way   way

west
서쪽

[west 웨스트]

west   west   west   west

zero
0, 영

[zíərou 지로우]

zero   zero   zero   zero

- Can you visit me, today?   오늘 절 방문해 줄 수 있나요?
- The sun sets in the west.   해는 서쪽으로 진다.
- There is no way through.   통로가 없어요.
- '0' is called zero.   0은 영이라고 부른다.

18. 육지 · 숲

country
나라, 지역
[kʌ́ntri 컨츠뤼]

country country country

field
들판
[fi:ld 퓌-ㄹ드]

field field field field

gold
금
[gould 고울드]

gold gold gold gold

green
녹색
[gri:n 그뤼인]

green green green green

· My grandmother lives in the country.　　할머니는 시골에서 사셔요.

· The farmer works in the field.　　농부가 들판에서 일을 해요.

· This box is full of gold.　　이 상자는 금으로 가득 차 있어요.

· I like green color.　　저는 녹색을 좋아해요.

ground
땅, 운동장

[graund
그라운드]

ground　　　ground

hill
언덕

[hil 힐]

hill　hill　hill　hill　hill　hill

island
섬

[áilənd아일런드]

island island　island

jungle
밀림, 정글

[dʒʌ́ŋgl쥐ㅇ글]

jungle jungle jungle jungle

land
땅, 육지

[lænd 랜드]

land land land land

- Let's play at the ground.   운동장에서 놀자.
- A cottage is on a hill.   언덕 위에 작은집이 하나 있다.
- I traveld over land and sea last year.   나는 작년에 육지와 바다를 여행했다.
- I have never been to the island.   나는 그 섬에 가본 적이 없어요.
- The lion is king of the jungle.   사자는 밀림의 왕이에요.

leaf
나뭇잎

[liːf 리-프]

leaf leaf leaf leaf leaf leaf

pool
웅덩이, 연못

[puːl 푸-울]

pool pool pool pool pool

rain
비, 비가오다

[rein 뢰인]

rain rain rain rain

wood
나무, 숲

[wud 우드]

wood wood wood wood

world
세계, 지구

[wəːrld 워-ㄹ드]

world world world world

- Look! The red leaf is falling.   봐봐! 빨간 나뭇잎이 떨어지고 있어.
- Fish are in the pool.   연못에 물고기들이 있어요.
- I walked in the rain.   나는 빗속을 걸었어요.
- I walked in the wood.   나는 숲속을 걸었어요.
- I want to travel all over the world.   나는 전 세계를 여행하고 싶다.

19. 인간의 삶

course
진로, 과정
[kɔːrs 코-ㄹ스]

course   course   course

god
하느님
[gad 가드]

god   god   god   god   god

group
무리, 모임, 떼
[gruːp 구류웁]

group group group

king
왕
[kiŋ 킹]

king   king   king

- The full course is finished now.　　　전 과정이 이제 끝났어요.
- Oh, God.　　　오, 신이시여.
- Each group has its flag.　　　각 그룹마다 깃발이 있어요.
- The lion is the king of animals.　　　사자는 동물의 왕이에요.

lead
인도하다

[iːd 리드]

lead   lead   lead   lead

letter
편지

[létər 레러-ㄹ]

letter   letter   letter   letter

life
생명, 생활

[laif 라이프]

life life life life life life

live
살다

[liv 리브]

live   live   live   live   live

luck
행운

[lɔk 럭]

luck   luck   luck   luck

- Lead him to the place.   그를 그 장소로 인도하시오.
- I send a letter to my friend Min-su.   나는 친구 민수에게 편지를 보내요.
- Thank you for saving my life.   제 생명을 구해주셔서 감사해요.
- Where do you live?   사시는 곳이 어디예요?
- Good luck!   행운을 빌어요!

mail
우편

[meil 메일]

mail　mail　mail

marry
결혼하다

[mǽri 매뤼]

marry　marry　marry　marry

men
man의 복수형

[men 멘]

men　men　men

news
소식

[njuːz 뉴-즈]

news　news　news

party
파티, 모임

[páːrti 파-ㄹ리]

party　party　party　party

- I send a letter by mail.　　나는 편지를 우편으로 보낸다.
- He will marry a woderful woman.　　그는 멋진 여성과 결혼할 것이다.
- Most men like playing football.　　대부분의 남자들은 축구하는 것을 좋아한다.
- Did you hear the news?　　그 소식 들었어?
- Can you come to my party?　　내 파티에 올래?

peace
평화

[piːs 피-스]

peace peace peace peace

queen
여왕

[kwiːn 퀴이-ㄴ]

queen queen queen

sleep
잠자다

[sliːp 슬리-입]

sleep sleep sleep sleep

village
마을, 촌락

[vílidʒ 빌리쥐]

village village village

welcome
환영하다

[wélkəm 웰컴]

welcome welcome

- I want the world peace.　　　　나는 세계 평화를 원한다.
- A queen is the wife of a king.　여왕은 왕의 아내이다.
- I went to sleep at 9 o'clock.　나는 9시에 잤어요.
- The farmer lives in the village.　그 농부는 마을에 살아요.
- Welcome to Korea!　　　　　한국에 오신 걸 환영합니다!

20. 숫 자

four
4, 4의
[fɔːr 포-]

four four four four four

half
반, 2분의1
[hæf 해프]

half half half half half

hour
시간
[auər 아우월]

hour hour hour

hundred
백(100)
[hʌndrəd헌드뤳]

hundred hundred

- **My family is** four.   우리 가족은 4명입니다.
- **Please cut this bread in** half.   이 빵을 반으로 잘라주세요.
- **Peter slept for five** hours.   Peter는 5시간동안 잤어요.
- **My grandfather is one** hundred **years old.** 할아버지는 100세이십니다.

21. 언제 · 누가 · 왜

and
그리고, ~와
[ænd 앤드]

and and and and and

ask
묻다, 질문하다
[æsk 애스크]

ask ask ask ask

because
왜냐하면
[bikɔ́ːz 비커-즈]

because because because

but
그러나, 하지만
[bʌt 벗]

but but but but but

- I like hamburger and pizza.   나는 햄버거와 피자를 좋아해.
- "What are you doing?" Mom asked.   "뭐하고 있니?" 엄마가 물어보셨어요.
- I like Tom because he is kind.   나는 Tom이 좋아요. 왜냐하면 친절하니까요.
- He likes apples. But I don't.   그는 사과를 좋아해요. 그러나 저는 안 좋아해요.

bye
(헤어질 때)안녕

[bai 바이]

bye bye bye bye

dictionary
사전

[díkʃəneri
딕셔네뤼]

dictionary dictionary

example
보기, 예

[igzǽmpl
이그젬쁠]

example example example

hear
듣다

[hiər 히얼]

hear hear hear hear

hello
안녕, 여보세요

[helóu 헬로우]

hello hello hello

- "Good bye~ see you later."　　　　"안녕~ 다음에 보자"
- Can I borrow your dictionary?　　당신의 사전을 빌릴 수 있을까요?
- Can you give me an example?　　예를 하나 들어볼래?
- Can you hear me?　　　　　　　내말 들리니?
- "Hello, may I speak to Tom?"　　여보세요, tom이랑 통화할 수 있을까요?

74

how
어떻게, 얼마나
[hau 하우]

how   how   how   how

idea
생각
[aidíːə 아이디어]

idea idea idea idea

listen
듣다
[lísn 리쓴]

listen   listen   listen   listen

matter
문제, 곤란
[mǽtər 매터]

matter   matter   matter

question
질문
[kwéstʃən 퀘스천]

question   question

- How are you?   어떻게 지내니?
- Do you have any ideas?   무슨 좋은 생각 있어?
- I listen to the music everyday.   나는 매일 음악을 듣는다.
- What is the matter with you?   무슨 일이야?
- Please answer my question.   질문에 대답해 주세요.

quiz
질문, 퀴즈

[kwíz 퀴즈]

quiz quiz quiz quiz

read
읽다, 낭독하다

[riːd 뤼-드]

read read read read

say
말하다

[sei 세이]

say say say say say say

speak
말하다

[spiːk 스삑-ㅋ]

speak speak speak speak

spell
철자

[spel 스뻴]

spell spell spell spell

- I'll give you a quiz.
- I read a book loudly.
- Don't say no.
- I can speak English.
- How do you spell this word?

내가 퀴즈 하나 낼께요.
나는 책을 큰소리로 읽었다.
안 된다고 말하지 마세요.
나는 영어를 말할 수 있어요.
이 단어의 철자가 어떻게 되나요?

76

story
이야기

[stɔ́:ri 스토뤼]

story　story　story　story

talk
말하다

[tɔ:k 터-억]

talk　talk　talk　talk

tell
말하다

[tel 텔]

tell　tell　tell　tell　tell　tell

think
~라고 생각하다

[θiŋk 씽크]

think　think　think　think

what
무엇, 어떤

[hwat 왓]

what　what　what

- Mom likes to tell me some stories.　엄마는 나에게 얘기해 주시는 걸 좋아하신다.
- What are you talking about?　너네 무슨 얘기하는 중이야?
- Don't tell a lie.　거짓말을 하지 마라.
- I think it is wrong.　나는 그것이 틀렸다고 생각한다.
- What are you doing?　뭐하고 있니?

when
언제

[*h*wen 웬]

when when when when

where
어디에

[*h*wɛər웨얼]

where where where

which
어느쪽, 어느

[*h*witʃ 윗취]

which which which which

who
누구

[*h*uː 후-]

who who who who

whom
누구를

[*h*uːm 후우-ㅁ]

whom whom whom whom

- When is your birthday?   생일이 언제야?
- Where are you from?   어디 출신이야?
- Which one is better?   어떤게 더 좋아?
- Who is he?   그는 누구야?
- Whom did you meet yesterday? 어제 누구를 만났어?

whose
누구의

[hu:z 후-즈]

whose whose whose

why
왜

[hwai 와이]

why   why   why   why

word
낱말, 단어

[wəːrd 워드]

word   word   word   word

yes
예, 네

[jes 예스]

yes

yes   yes   yes   yes

- Whose **daughter is she?**　　　누구의 딸이야?
- Why **do you cry?**　　　왜 우니?
- **How do you spell this** word**?**　　　이 단어 철자가 어떻게 되죠?
- Yes**, ma'am.**　　　네, 선생님

79

22. 움직임을 나타내는 단어(동사)

break
부수다

[breik브뢰익크]

break break break break

---

broke
깨트렸다

[brouk브로-크]

broke broke broke broke

---

build
세우다, 짓다

[bild 빌드]

build build build build

---

burn
타다, 태우다

[bəːrn버-ㄹ언]

burn burn burn burn

- A glass is easy to break.　　유리는 깨지기 쉽다.
- I broke my grandma's glasses.　　내가 할머니의 안경을 깨트렸다.
- I want to build a doghouse.　　나는 개집을 짓고 싶어요.
- Mom burned the steaks today.　　엄마는 오늘 스테이크를 태웠어요.

call
부르다

[kɔːl 커얼]

call call call call

carry
운반하다

[kǽri 캐뤼]

carry carry carry carry

catch
잡다, 받다

[kætʃ 캣취]

catch catch catch catch

close
닫다

[klouz 클로우즈]

close close close close

count
수를 세다

[kaunt 카운트]

count count count count

- My friends call me Sunny.
- I always carry schoolbag.
- Cats are very good at catching mice.
- Close one eye and look at that.
- Let's count to 10! 1, 2, 3...

친구들은 저를 Sunny라고 불러요.
저는 항상 책가방을 가지고 다녀요.
고양이는 쥐를 아주 잘 잡아요.
한쪽 눈을 감고 저것을 봐봐.
10까지 세어보자! 일, 이, 삼...

cut
베다, 깎다

[kʌt 컷]

cut　cut　cut　cut　cut

die
죽다

[dai 다이]

die　die　die　die　die

drink
마시다

[driŋk 쥬륑크]

drink　drink　drink

drive
운전하다

[draiv 드롸이브]

drive　drive　drive

enjoy
즐기다

[éndʒɔ́i 엔줘이]

enjoy　enjoy　enjoy

- I had cut my finger.　　나는 손가락을 베었다.
- That sick dog will die.　　저 아픈 개는 죽을거야.
- If you are thirsty, drink some water.　　목이 마르면 물을 좀 마시세요.
- Can you drive a car?　　차 운전할 줄 알아요?
- My dad enjoys driving.　　아빠는 운전을 즐기셔요.

82

excuse
용서하다

[ikskjú:z 익스큐즈]

excuse   excuse   excuse

fill
채우다

[fil 필]

fill fill fill fill fill fill

find
찾다, 발견하다

[faind 퐈인드]

find   find   find   find

fix
수리하다

[fiks 퓍ㄱ스]

fix fix fix fix fix fix

fly(1)
날다

[flai 플롸이]

fly fly fly fly fly

· The game excited us.　　　　　그 시합은 우리를 흥분시켰다.

· Fill in the blank.　　　　　　　빈칸을 채우세요.

· I can't find my doll.　　　　　제 인형을 찾을 수가 없어요.

· Dad and I will fix the roof today.　아빠랑 오늘 지붕을 고칠꺼에요.

· I can't fly.　　　　　　　　　나는 날 수 없어요.

fly(1)
날다

[flai 플롸이]

fly　fly　fly　fly　fly

have
가지고 있다

[hæv 해브]

have　have　have

help
돕다

[help 헬-프]

help　help　help

hit
때리다

[hit 힛]

hit　hit　hit　hit　hit　hit

hold
잡다, 붙들다

[hould 호울드]

hold　hold　hold　hold

- I can't fly.　　　　　　　　나는 날 수 없어요.
- I have a lot of stamps.　　저는 우표를 아주 많이 가지고 있어요.
- Help me, please!　　　　저를 도와주세요!
- Don't hit me!　　　　　　나를 때리지 마.
- "Hold my hand!", he cries.　"내 손을 잡아!" 그가 외쳤어요.

hope
바라다

[houp 호웁]

hope hope hope hope

hurt
다치게 하다

[hə:rt허-ㄹ트]

hurt hurt hurt hurt

keep
계속하다

[ki:p 키-입]

keep keep keep keep

kick
차다

[kik 킥]

kick kick kick kick

kill
죽이다, 없애다

[kil 킬]

kill kill kill kill kill kill

- I hope you have a good time.　　좋은 시간되시길 바랍니다.
- I am badly hurt.　　난 심하게 다쳤어요.
- Keep your room clean.　　당신의 방을 깨끗히 유지하세요.
- Tom kicked a ball.　　Tom은 공을 찼어요.
- Cats kill the mouse.　　고양이는 쥐를 죽여요.

knock
두드리다

[nak 낙]

knock knock knock

know
알다, 이해하다

[nou 노우]

know know know know

jump
뛰어오르다

[dʒʌmp 줘ㅁ프]

jump jump jump

like
좋아하다

[laik 라이크]

like like like like like

look
보다

[luk 룩]

look look look

- I knocked the door.
- Do you know what I mean?
- Teddy is ready to jump up.
- I like dancing.
- Look at it. Do you know what it is?

전 노크를 했어요.
내가 무슨 말 하는 지 알겠어?
Teddy는 뛰어오를 준비가 되었어요
저는 춤추는 걸 좋아해요.
이것 좀 봐. 이게 뭔지 알어?

leave
떠나다

[liːv 리-브]

love
사랑하다

[lʌv 러브]

make
만들다

[meik 메이크]

may
~해도 좋다

[mei 메이]

move
움직이다

[muːv 무-브]

- I leave at 3.
- Mom and dad love each other.
- Look at it. Do you know what it is?
- Mom and dad love each other.
- I made a cake for my mother.

나는 3시에 떠나요.
엄마 아빠는 서로를 사랑하셔요.
이것 좀 봐. 이게 뭔지 알어?
엄마 아빠는 서로를 사랑하셔요.
나는 어머니를 위해 케이크를 만들었어요.

pass
지나가다
[pæs 패스]

pass pass pass pass

pick
따다
[pik 픽]

pick pick pick pick

play
연주하다, 놀다
[plei 플레이]

play play play

please
기쁘게 하다
[pliːz플리이즈]

please please please

put
놓다, 두다
[put 풋]

put put put put put

- I passed through the park.
- Please, pick one of them.
- She plays the violin very well.
- I am pleased to see you.
- I put some flowers into the vase.

나는 공원을 가로질러 지나갔다.

그것들 중 하나를 고르세요.

그녀는 바이올린 연주를 매우 잘한다.

너를 보게 되어 기뻐.

꽃병에 꽃 몇 송이를 넣었다.

remember 기억하다 [rimémbər 뤼멤버얼]	remember remember
ride 타다 [raid 롸이드]	ride ride ride ride ride
ring 울리다 [riŋ 륑]	ring ring ring ring ring
run 달리다 [rʌn 뤄ㄴ]	run run run run
see 보다 [si: 씨-]	see see see see

- I remember her.   나는 그녀를 기억한다.
- Can you ride a bicycle?   자전거 탈 줄 아니?
- The telephone is ringing.   전화가 울리고 있어요.
- I like to run.   나는 달리는 걸 좋아해요.
- I want to see you!   네가 보고싶어!

send
보내다

[send 쎈드]

send   send   send   send

show
보이다

[ʃou 쇼우]

show   show   show   show

slide
미끄러지다

[slaid슬라이드]

slide   slide   slide   slide

smell
냄새맡다

[smel 스멜]

smell   smell   smell   smell

strike
때리다

[straik스뜨롸익]

strike   strike   strike   strike

- I will send you an e-mail.　　　나는 너에게 e-mail을 보낼 것이다.
- Can you show it to me?　　　그것을 내게 보여줄 수 있니?
- She slid on the ice.　　　그녀는 얼음판 위에서 미끄러졌다.
- It smells good.　　　좋은 냄새가 난다.
- i strike a ball.　　　나는공을 찬다.

23. 모양을 나타내는 단어(형용사)

angry
화난
[ǽŋgri 앵그뤼]

angry   angry   angry

any
무엇이든
[éni 애니]

any   any   any   any   any

beautiful
아름다운
[bjúːtəfəl
뷰-러플]

beautiful   beautiful

broken
부러진
[broukən브뤄큰]

broken   broken   broken

· Don be angry with ne.   나한테 화내지마.

· Do you have any questions?   무슨 질문이 있나요?

· Snow white is beautiful.   백설공주는 예뻐요.

· I have broken my arm. a ball.   팔이 부러졌어.

busy
바쁜

[bízì 비지]

busy   busy   busy

careful
조심스러운

[kέərfəl
캐어ㄹ풀]

careful   careful   careful

close
가까운, 친한

[klous클로우즈]

close   close   close   close

dead
죽은

[ded 데드]

dead   dead   dead   dead

empty
텅 빈

[émpti엠티]

empty empty empty

- My parents are busy.
- Be careful not to drop the cup.
- Tom and Jerry are very close friends.
- My cat was dead.
- The room is empty.

우리 부모님은 바쁘셔요.
컵을 떨어뜨리지 않게 조심해.
Tom과 Jerry는 아주 친한 친구 사이예요.
제 고양이가 죽었어요.
그 방은 비었어요.

every
모든
[évriː 에브뤼]

every every every

fair
공평한, 공정한
[fɛər 페얼]

fair fair fair fair fair

few
거의 없는
[fjuː 퓨-]

few few few few

foolish
어리석은
[fúːliʃ 푸-울리쉬]

foolish foolish foolish

free
자유로운
[friː 프뤼-]

free free free free

- Everyone likes him.　　　　　　　　모두 그를 좋아해요.
- I think it was a fair game.　　　　공정한 게임이었다고 생각해요.
- I have few cards.　　　　　　　　나는 카드도 별로 없어요.
- It was a foolish idea.　　　　　　그건 어리석은 생각이었어요.
- What do you do in your free time?　한가할 때 뭐하세요?

full

가득한, 충만한

[ful 풀]

full full full full

good

좋은, 착한

[gud 굿]

good good good good

hard

딱딱한, 어려운

[haːrd 하알드]

hard hard hard hard

hungry

배고픈

[hʌ́ŋgri 헝그뤼]

hungry hungry

ill

아픈, 병든

[il 일]

ill ill ill ill ill ill ill ill ill

· The box is full of books.　　　　이 박스에는 책이 가득 들어있다.

· I think it is a good idea.　　　　좋은 생각인 것 같아요.

· It is very hard to solve this problem.　이 문제를 해결하는 건 어려워요.

· I'm very hungry.　　　　　　　나 정말 배고파요.

· Teddy is ill in bed.　　　　　Teddy는 아파서 누워있어요.

kind
친절한
[kaind 카인드]

kind   kind   kind   kind

late
늦은, 늦게
[leit 레잇]

late   late   late   late

lonely
외로운
[lóunlí 로운리]

lonely lonely lonely lonely

loud
목소리가 큰
[laud 라우드]

loud   loud   loud   loud

mad
미친, 열광한
[mæd 매드]

mad   mad   mad   mad

- The police officer is very kind.
- Let's meet at 7 o'clock. Don't be late.
- I feel lonely.
- He has a loud voice.
- He is mad about games.

그 경찰관은 매우 친절해요.

7시에 만나자. 늦지마!

나는 외롭다.

그는 목소리가 커요.

그는 게임에 열중해 있다.

95

new
새로운
[nju: 뉴-]

new　new　new

next
다음의, 다음에
[nekst 넥스트]

next　next　next　next

nice
멋진
[nais 나이스]

nice　nice　nice　nice

no
하나도 없는
[nóu 노우]

no　no　no　no　no　no

only
오직, 유일한
[óunli 오운리]

only　only　only　only

. I wear a new uniform.　　　나는 새로운 교복을 입는다.
· See you next time.　　　다음에 보자.
· This jacket is very nice.　　이 자켓은 매우 멋져요.
· There are no one in the room.　방엔 아무도 없어요.
· This jacket is very nice.　　이 자켓은 매우 멋져요.

I wear a new uniform.

See you next time.

quiet
조용한

[kwáiət 콰이엇-트]

quiet quiet

quiet

safe
안전한

[seif 쎄이프]

safe   safe   safe   safe

stupid
어리석은

[stjú:pid스뚜피-드]

stupid stupid stupid stupid

thank
감사하다

[θæŋk 쌩크]

thank thank thank

wet
젖은, 축축한

[wet 웨트]

wet   wet   wet   wet

- Be quiet!   조용히 해!
- There is a safe place.   안전한 장소다.
- He is stupid.   그는 어리석다.
- Thank you very much.   정말 감사합니다.
- We have the wet season in June.   6월은 장마철이다.

24. 대립어

in
~안에
[in 인]

in in in in in in

out
밖으로, 밖에
[aut 아웃]

out out out out out

push
밀다
[puʃ 푸쉬]

push push push push

pull
당기다
[pul 풀]

pull pull pull pull

- There is a cat in the box.　　　상자 안에 고양이 한 마리가 있다.
- Let's go out.　　　우리 밖으로 나가자.
- Push the door open.　　　문을 밀어서 열어요.
- Pull the door open.　　　문을 당겨서 열어요.

sit
앉다

[sit 씻]

sit   sit   sit   sit   sit

stand
서다, 일어서다

[stænd스팬드]

stand   stand   stand   stand

open
열다

[óupən 오우쁜]

open   open   open

shut
닫다, 덮다

[ʃʌt 셧]

shut   shut   shut   shut

- Sit down, please.
- Stand up, please.
- Open the door, please.
- Please shut the window.

앉아 주세요.

일어서 주세요.

문좀 열어 주세요.

창문 좀 닫아 주세요.

glad
기쁜, 반가운
[glæd 글래드]

glad　glad　glad　glad

sad
슬 픈
[sǽd 쌔에드]

sad　sad　sad　sad

fine
좋은
[fain 퐈인]

fine　fine　fine　fine　fine

bad
나쁜
[bǽd 베드]

bad　bad　bad　bad

- I'm glad to meet you.　　　　만나서 반가워.
- She looks sad.　　　　　　　그녀는 슬퍼보여.
- The weather is fine, today.　오늘 날씨가 좋아요.
- I feel bad today.　　　　　　난 오늘 기분이 나빠.

large
큰

[lɑːrdʒ 라-ㄹ쥐]

large   large   large   large

small
작은

[smɔːl 스모-ㄹ]

small   small   small   small

thin
얇은

[θin 띤]

thin   thin   thin   thin

thick
두꺼운

[θik 씩]

thick   thick   thick

- I want large size skirt.　　　　전 큰 사이즈 치마를 원해요.
- The ball is small.　　　　　　그 공은 작다.
- This book is very thin.　　　　이 책은 정말 얇아요.
- How thick is it?　　　　　　　그건 두께가 얼마나 되죠?

fat
뚱뚱한
[fæt 퓌앳]

fat fat fat fat fat fat fat

thin
얇은
[θin 띤]

thin thin thin thin thin

heavy
무거운
[hévi 헤뷔]

heavy heavy heavy

light(1)
가벼운
[lait 라잇트]

light light light

- My cat is little fat, but very cute.　우리 고양이는 조금 뚱뚱하지만 귀여워요.
- She is very thin.　그녀는 매우 날씬해요.
- Elephants are really heavy.　코끼리는 아주 무겁다.
- Tom is lighter than his brother.　Tom은 그의 형보다 가벼워요.

quick
빠른

[kwik 퀵]

quick   quick   quick   quick

slow
느린

[slou 슬로우]

slow   slow   slow

much
많은

[mʌtʃ 멋취]

much   much   much   much

little
약간의

[litl 리를]

little   little   little   little

- He is quick to learn.　　　　　그는 배우는 속도가 빠르다.
- The turtle is slow.　　　　　　거북이는 느리다.
- Don't spend too much money.　돈을 너무 많이 쓰지 마세요.
- I have a little hope.　　　　　나에게는 약간의 희망이 있어.

103

little
작은

[litl 리틀]

little little little little

big
큰, 커다란

[big 빅]

big big big big

left
왼쪽, 왼쪽의

[left 레프트]

left left left left

right
오른쪽

[rait 롸잇트]

right right right

- Tom is walking with the little boy.　　Tom이 작은 소년과 걷고 있어요.

- An elephant is a big animal.　　코끼리는 몸집이 큰 동물이예요.

- Turn left there.　　저기서 왼쪽으로 도세요.

- Turn right.　　오른쪽으로 도세요.

down
아래로

[daun 다운]

down down down down

up
위쪽으로

[ʌp 엎]

up up up up up up up

young
젊은, 어린

[jʌŋ 영]

young young young young

old
늙은

[ould 오울드]

old old old old old old

- I went down the stairs. 나는 계단을 내려갔어요.
- Stand up please. 일어서 주세요.
- He is young. 그는 어리다.
- How old are you? 몇 살이지요?

end
끝, 마치다
[end 엔드]

end end end end end

begin
시작하다
[begín 비긴]

begin begin begin

come
오다
[kʌm 컴]

come come come come

go
가다
[gou 고우]

go go go go go

- This is the end.   이것으로 끝이다.
- Our class begins at 8.   수업은 8시에 시작한다.
- Grandfather will come next Friday.   할아버지는 다음주 금요일날 오실꺼에요.
- I go to school everyday.   나는 매일 학교에 간다.

true

진실의

[trú: 트루]

true   true   true   true

false

거짓의

[fɔ́ːls 폴스]

false   false   false   false

far

멀리

[faːr 퐈-ㄹ]

far   far   far   far   far

near

가까운

[niər 니얼]

near   near   near   near

- It is true.   사실이야.
- The rumor was false.   그 소문은 거짓이었어.
- My house is far from here.   우리집은 여기서 멀어요.
- Our house stands near my school.   우리집은 학교 옆에 있어요.

start
출발하다

[staːrt 스딸-트]

start start start start

stop
멈추다

[stap 스땁]

stop stop stop stop

high
높은

[hái 하이]

high high high high

low
낮은

[lóu 로우]

low low low low low

- Let's start. 시작하자
- He stopped to talk. 그는 이야기하기 위해 멈췄다.
- Mt. Everest is really high. 에베레스트 산은 정말 높아요.
- The temperature is low today. 오늘은 기온이 낮다.

great
큰, 엄청난

[greit 그뤠잇]

great   great   great   great

little
작은

[lítl 리를]

little   little   little   little

fine
좋은

[fain 퐈인]

fine   fine   fine   fine

bad
나쁜

[bǽd 베드]

bad   bad   bad   bad

- I heard some great news!   나 엄청난 소식을 들었어!
- Tom is walking with the little boy.   Tom이 작은 소년과 걷고 있어요.
- The weather is fine, today.   오늘 날씨가 좋아요.
- I feel bad today.   난 오늘 기분이 나빠.

Tom is walking with the little boy.   Tom이 작은 소년과 걷고 있어요.

warm
따뜻한
[wɔːrm 워-ㄹ엄]

warm warm warm

cold
추운
[kóuld 코울드]

cold cold cold

long
긴
[lɔ́ːŋ 러-엉]

long long long

short
짧은
[ʃɔ́ːrt 쇼올트]

short short short

- Today is warm.   오늘은 따뜻하다.
- It's cold in winter.   겨울은 추워요.
- A giraffe has a long neck.   기린은 목이 길어요.
- She likes to wear short skirt.   그녀는 짧은 치마 입는 것을 좋아해.

hate
싫어하다

[heit 헤잇트]

hate   hate   hate   hate

like
좋아하다

[láik 라익]

like   like   like   like   like

hot
더운, 뜨거운

[hat 핫]

hot   hot   hot   hot   hot

cool
시원한

[kúːl 쿠울]

cool   cool   cool

- I hate mouse.   난 쥐를 싫어해.
- Sally likes you.   셀리가 널 좋아해.
- I don't like hot weather.   나는 더운 날씨를 별로 안 좋아해요.
- I want to drink cool water.   나 시원한 물이 마시고 싶어.

easy
쉬운
[íːzi 이-지]

easy   easy   easy   easy

difficult
어려운
[dífikʌlt 디퓌컬트]

difficult   difficult   difficult

into
~안으로
[intu 인투]

into   into   into   into

outside
밖에
[áutsáid
아웃사이드]

outside   outside

- It's easy to say "Thank you."   고맙다고 말하는 건 쉬워요.
- That is so difficult problem to solve.   저건 풀기에 너무 어려운 문제야.
- Jim went into his house.   Jim은 그의 집으로 들어갔어요.
- It's a lovely day outside.   밖에 날씨가 너무 좋아요.

happy
행복한

[hǽpi 해삐]

happy happy happy

unhappy
불행한

[ʌ̀nhǽpi 언해삐]

unhappy　　　　unhappy

different
다른

[dífərənt
디퍼런트]

different　　　different

equal
같은

[íːkwəl 이쿠얼]

equal equal equal equal

- I'm happy to be with you.　　　너랑 있어 행복해.
- She was unhappy about the news.　　그녀는 그 소식에 슬픈 생각이 들었다.
- I need a different pen.　　나 다른 펜이 필요해.
- Ducks are equal in size.　　오리들은 크기가 같다.

113

deep
깊은
[diːp 디-입]

deep   deep   deep

low
얕은
[lóu 로우]

take
받다
[teik 테익]

take   take   take   take

give
주다
[gív 기브]

give   give   give

- How deep is the river?   강이 얼마나 깊나요?
- The stream was so low that we could cross it.   개울가가 얕아서 우리가 건널 수 있었다.
- Take this letter to your mother.   이 편지를 어머니께 가져다 드리렴.
- Please, give me that book.   그 책을 좀 줘.

fast
빠른

[fæst 풰 스트]

fast fast fast fast

slow
느린

[slóu 슬로우]

slow slow slow slow

expensive
비싼

[ikspénsiv 익스펜시브]

expensive expensive

cheap
값이 싼, 싸게

[tʃiːp 취-입]

cheap cheap cheap cheap

- It is very fast train.   이건 굉장히 빠른 기차예요.
- Will you slow down?   좀 천천히 할래?
- Isn't this pretty expensive?   이거 꽤 비싸지 않아?
- The candy was very cheap.   그 사탕은 값이 쌌어요.

sell
팔다

[sel 쎌]

sell sell sell sell sell sell

buy
사다, 구입하다

[bai 바이]

buy buy buy buy buy buy

many
많은

[méni 매니]

many many many

few
약간의

[fju: 퓨-]

few few few few few

- He sells cars.   그는 자동차를 판다.
- I buy some chocolate at the store.   나는 가게에서 초콜릿을 삽니다.
- He has many friends.   그는 친구들이 많아요.
- I have few cards.   나는 카드도 별로 없어요.

tall
키가 큰

[tɔːl 토-ㄹ]

tall　tall　tall　tall　tall

short
짧은, 키가작은

[ʃɔːrt 쇼-ㄹ트]

short　short　short　short

best
가장 좋은

[best 베스트]

best　best　best

worst
최악의

[wə́ːrst 워어ㄹ스트]

worst　worst　worst　worst

- He is tall.　　　　　　　　　　그는 키가 크다.
- She likes to wear short skirt.　그녀는 짧은 치마 입는 것을 좋아해.
- I did my best.　　　　　　　　나는 최선을 다했어요.
- She was the worst singer.　　그녀는 최악의 가수였어.

dirty
더러운, 불결한

[dɔ́ːrti 더-ㄹ리]

dirty dirty dirty dirty dirty

clean
깨끗한

[kliːn 클리인]

clean clean clean

great
큰, 엄청난

[greit 그뤠잇]

great great great great

little
작은

[litl 리를]

little little little little

- My brother's room is dirty all the time.   내 동생 방은 항상 더러워요.
- I clean my room everyday.   저는 제방을 매일 청소해요.
- I heard some great news!   나 엄청난 소식을 들었어!
- Tom is walking with the little boy.   Tom이 작은 소년과 걷고 있어요.

wide
넓은

[waid 와이드]

wide   wide   wide

narrow
좁은

[nǽrou 내로오우]

narrow   narrow   narrow

lot
많음

[lat 랏]

lot lot lot lot lot lot

few
거의 없는

[fjúː 퓨]

few   few   few   few   few

- That place is wide.　　　　　　　　그곳은 넓어요.
- He jumped a narrow stream.　　　　그는 좁은 개울을 뛰어넘었어.
- There are a lot of people on the beach.　해변에 사람이 많아요.
- I have few books.　　　　　　　　　나는 책이 거의 없어.

🎒 찾아보기

cheese 치즈(17)

chicken 닭(24)

church 교회(54)

city 도시(54)

class 수업, 학급(5)

clean 깨끗한(118)

close 닫다(92)

cloud 구름(20)

club 클럽, 동호회(8)

coat 외투(51)

cold 추운(110)

color 색깔(28)

come 오다(106)

computer 컴퓨터(5)

cool 시원한(111)

corn 옥수수(17)

count 수를 세다(81)

country 나라, 지역 (65)

course 진로, 과정 (68)

cow 암소, 젖소(25)

crayon 크레용(5)

cream 크림(17)

cucumber 오이(14)

cup 컵(44)

curtain 커튼(44)

cut 베다, 깎다(82)

d

dance 춤, 춤추다(9)

date 날짜(59)

day 낮, 하루(59)

dead 죽은(92)

deep 깊은(114)

deer 사슴(25)

desk 책상(5)

dictionary 사전(74)

die 죽다(82)

difficult 어려운, 다른 (112,113)

dinner 저녁 식사(17)

dirty 더러운, 불결한 (118)

dish 접시(44)

door 문(44)

down 아래로(105)

dress 의복(51)

drink 마시다(82)

drive 운전하다(82)

drum 북, 드럼(9)

e

ear 귀(39)

earth 지구, 땅(20)

east 동쪽(63)

easy 쉬운(112)

egg 달걀(18)

elephant 코끼리(25)

empty 텅 빈(92)

end 끝, 마치다(106)

enjoy 즐기다(82)

equal 같은(113)

eraser 지우개(5)

evening 저녁(60)

every 모든(93)

excuse 용서하다(83)

exercise 운동, 연습(9)

expensive 비싼(115)

eye 눈(40)

f

face 얼굴(40)

fair 공평한, 공정한 (93)

fall 가을(60)

false 거짓의(107)

far 멀리(107)

fast 빠른(115)

fat 뚱뚱한(102)

few거의 없는 (18,93,119)

field 들판(65)

fill 채우다(83)

film 필름, 영화(9)

find 찾다, 발견하다 (83)

fine 좋은(100,109)

finger 손가락(40)

fish 물고기(25)

fix 수리하다(83)

floor 바닥, 층(54)

fly(1) 날다(84)

fly(2) 파리(26)

food 음식(18)

foolish 어리석은(93)

foot 발(40)

fox 여우(26)

frree 자유로운(93)

fruit 과일(14)

full 가득한, 충만한 (94)

g

game 게임·놀이(9)

arden 정원(45)

gas 가스(45)

give 주다(114)

glad 기쁜, 반가운 (100)

glass 유리, 유리컵 (45)

go 가다(106)

god 하느님(68)

gold 금(65)

good 좋은, 착한(94)

grape 포도(14)

grass 풀(21)

gray 회색, 회색의(29)

great 큰, 엄청난 (109,118)

green 녹색(65)

ground 땅, 운동장(66)

group 무리, 모임, 떼 (68)

guitar 기타(10)

h

hair 머리카락, 털(40)

hamburger 햄버거 (18)

hand 손(41)

happy 행복한(113)

hard 딱딱한, 어려운 (94)

hate 싫어하다(111)

have 가지고 있다(84)

he 그는, 그가(30)

head 머리(41)

hear 듣다(74)

heart 마음, 심장(41)

heavy 무거운(102)

hello 안녕, 여보세요 (74)

help 돕다(84)

hen 암탉(26)

her 그녀의(30)

hers 그녀의 것(30)

high 높은(106)

hill 언덕(66)

him 그를, 그에게(30)

his 그의, 그의 것(31)

hit 때리다(84)

hold잡다, 붙들다(84)

home 집(45)

hope 바라다(85)

horse 말(26)

hospital 병원(54)

hot 더운, 뜨거운(111)

hotel 호텔(54)

hour 시간(60)

how 어떻게, 얼마나 (75)

hungry 배고픈(94)

hurt 다치게 하다(85)

i

I 나는, 내가(31)

idea 생각(75)

ill 아픈, 병든(94)

in ~안에(98)

into ~안으로(112)

island 섬(66)

it 그것은(31)

its 그것의(31)

j

Juice 주스(18)

jump 뛰어오르다(86)

jungle 밀림, 정글(66)

k

keep 계속하다(85)

kick 차다(85)

kill 죽이다, 없애다 (85)

kind 친절한(95)

king 왕(68)

kitchen 부엌(45)

knee 무릎(41)

knife 칼(46)

knock 두드리다(86)

know알다,이해하다 (86)

l

lake 호수(21)

land 땅, 육지(66)

large 큰(101)

last 마지막으로(95)

lead 인도하다(69)

leaf 나뭇잎(67)

learn 배우다(6)

left 왼쪽, 왼쪽의 (104)

leg 다리(41)

lesson 수업(6)

letter 편지(69)

library 도서관(6)

life 생명, 생활(69)

light 가벼운(102)

like 좋아하다(86,111)

lip 입술(42)

listen 듣다(75)

little 약간의 (103,104,109,118)

live 살다(69)

lonely 외로운(95,96)

long 긴(110)

look 보다(86)

lot 많음(119)

loud 목소리가 큰 (95,96)

love 사랑하다(87)

low 낮은(108,114)

luck 행운(69)

lunch 점심(60)

m

mad 미친, 열광한 (95,96)

mail 우편(70)

make 만들다(87)

many 많은(116)

map 지도(63)

marry 결혼하다(70)

matter 문제, 곤란(75)

may ~해도 좋다(87)

me 나를(31)

meat 고기(18)

melon 메론(114)

men man의 복수형 (70)

milk 우유(19)

mine 나의 것(32)

mirror 거울(46)

mom 엄마(38)

monkey 원숭이(26)

morning 아침(60)

mother 어머니(38)

mountain 산(21)

mouth 입(42)

move 움직이다(87)

movie 영화(10)

music 음악(10)

my 나의(32)

n

narrow 좁은(119)

near 가까운(107)

neck 목(42)

new 새로운(96)

news 소식(70)

next 다음의, 다음에 (96)

night 밤(61)

no 하나도 없는(98)

noon 정오, 한 낮(61)

north 북쪽(63)

nose 코(42)

o

office 사무실(55)

old 늙은(105)

onion 양파(14)

only 오직, 유일한(97)

open 열다(99)

our 우리의(32)

ours 우리의 것(32)

out 밖으로, 밖에(98)

outside 밖에(112)

p

page 페이지, 쪽(6)

pants 바지(51)

party 파티, 모임(70)

pass 지나가다(88)

peace 평화(71)

peach 복숭아(15)

pear (과일)배(15)

piano 피아노(10)

pick 따다(88)

picnic 소풍(55)

pig 돼지(27)

pin 핀(6)

pineapple 파인애풀 (15)

pink 분홍(29)

place 장소, 곳(55)

plant 식물(21)

play 연주하다, 놀다 (88)

please 기쁘게 하다 (89)

pool 웅덩이, 연못 (67)

pull 당기다(98)

push 밀다(98)

put 놓다, 두다(88)

q

queen 여왕(71)

question 질문(75)

quick 빠른(103)

quiet 조용한(97)

quiz 질문, 퀴즈(76)

r

rain 비, 비가오다(67)

rainbow 무지개(21)

read 읽다, 낭독하다 (76)

red 빨간색, 붉은(29)

remember 기억하다(89)

restaurant 레스토랑 (55)

rice 쌀, 밥(19)

ride 타다(89)

right 오른쪽(104)

ring 울리다(89)

ring 반지(52)

river 강(22)

road 길, 도로(55)

roof 지붕(46)

room 방(46)

run 달리다(89)

s

sad 슬픈(100)

safe 안전한(97)

salad 샐러드(19)

salt 소금(19)

sand 모래(22)

say 말하다(76)

school 학교, 수업(7)

sea 바다(22)

season 계절(61)

see 보다(89)

sell 팔다(116)

send 보내다(90)

she 그녀는, 그녀가(32)

sheep 양(27)

ship 배(58)

shoe 신, 구두(52)

short 짧은(110,117)

show 보이다(90)

shut 닫다, 덮다(99)

silver 은, 은빛, 은의 (22)

sing 노래, 노래하다 (10)

sister 여자형제, 언니 (38)

sit 앉다(99)

skate 스케이트(11)

skirt 스커트(52)

sled 썰매(58)

sleep 잠자다(71)

slide 미끄러지다(90)

slow 느린(103,115)

small 작은(101)

smell 냄새맡다(90)

snow 눈, 눈이오다 (22)

soap 비누(46)

soccer 축구(11)

sofa 소파(47)

son 아들(38)

song 노래(11)

south 남쪽(63)

space 공간, 우주(23)

speak 말하다(76)

spell 철자(76)

spoon 숟가락, 스푼 (47)

sport 스포츠(11)

spring 봄(61)

stair 계단(47)

stamp 우표, 인지(72)

stand 서다, 일어서다 (99)

star 별(23)

start 출발하다(108)

station 역, 정거장 (56)

stop 멈추다(108)

story 이야기(77)

strawberry 딸기(15)

street 거리(56)

strike 때리다(90)

student 학생(71)

study 공부하다(71)

subway 지하철(58)

sugar 설탕(19)

summer 여름(61)

sun 태양, 햇빛(23)

sweater 스웨터(52)

swim 수영하다, 수영 (11)

swing 그네(12)

t

table 테이블(7)

take 받다(114)

talk 말하다(77)

tall 키가 큰(117)

tteam 팀(72)

telephone 전화(47)

tell 말하다(77)

tennis 테니스(12)

test 시험, 검사(7)

that 저것, 그것(33)

the 그(33)

their 그들의(33)

them 그들을(33)

there 거기에(33)

these 이것들(34)

they 그들은(34)

thick 두꺼운(101)

thin 얇은(101,102)

think ~라고 생각하다 (77)

this 이것(34)

those 그것들(34)

tiger 호랑이(27)

today 오늘(62)

tomato 토마토(15)

tomorrow 내일(62)

tooth 이, 치아(42)

town 마을(72)

train 기차(58)

travel여행, 여행하다 (56)

trip 여행(56)

truck 트럭(58)

true 진실의(107)

u

umbrella 우산(52)

unhappy 불행한(113)

up 위쪽으로(105)

us 우리들을(34)

v

video 비디오(12)

village 마을, 촌락(72)

violin 바이올린(12)

visit 방문하다(64)

w

warm 따뜻한(110)

water 물(23)

way 길, 방법(64)

we 우리, 저희가(35)

week 주, 1주간(62)

welcome 환영하다(72)

west 서쪽(64)

what 무엇, 어떤(77)

when 언제(78)

where 어디에(78)

which 어느쪽, 어느(78)

white 흰, 흰빛(29)

who 누구(78)

whom 누구를(78)

whose 누구의(79)

why 왜(79)

wide 넓은(119)

wind 바람(23)

window 창(창문)(47)

winter 겨울(62)

wood 나무, 숲(67)

word 낱말, 단어(79)

world 세계, 지구(67)

worst 최악의(117)

y

year 년, 나이(64)

yellow 노랑(29)

yes 예, 네(79)

yesterday 어제(62)

you 너, 당신(35)

young 젊은, 어린(105)

your 너의, 너희들의(35)

yours 너의 것(35)

z

zero 0, 영(64)

zoo 동물원(27)

초등 영단어 500 따라쓰기

재판 3쇄 발행 2017년 9월 20일

글 Y&M 어학 연구소

펴낸이 서영희 | **펴낸곳** 와이 앤 엠

편집 임명아 | **책임교정** 하연정

본문인쇄 신화프린팅 | **제책** 일진 제책

제작 이윤식 | **마케팅** 강성태

주소 120-848 서울시 서대문구 홍은동 376-28

전화 (02)308-3891 | Fax (02)308-3892

E-mail yam3891@naver.com

등록 2007년 8월 29일 제312-2007-000040호

ISBN 978-89-93557-55-8   63740

본사는 출판물 윤리강령을 준수합니다.